THE DESERT LULLABY

THE DESERT LULLABY

A Play in Two Acts

JENNIFER JOHNSTON

LAGAN PRESS
BELFAST
1996

Published by
Lagan Press
PO Box 110 BT12 4AB, Belfast

The publishers wish to acknowledge the financial assistance of
the Arts Council of Northern Ireland in the production of this book.

ISBN: 1 873687 26 5
Author: Johnston, Jennifer
Title: The Desert Lullaby
Format: Paperback
1996

Cover: Stella McCusker
and Pauline Flanagan in *The Desert Lullaby*
Design: December Publications
Set in New Baskerville
Printed by Noel Murphy Printing, Belfast

To My Dear Friend
Dudley Sutton

THE DESERT LULLABY

The Desert Lullaby was first presented by the Lyric Players' Theatre, Belfast on 31st October, 1996. The play was directed by Caroline Fitzgerald. The cast was as follows:

Flora	Stella McCusker
Nellie	Pauline Flanagan
Young Flora	Lisa Harding
Young Nellie	Síle Nic Chonaonaigh
Eddie	Patrick Lennox

ACT ONE

It is a room, a terrace, an overgrown garden. The house dates from the late eighteenth century, so the proportions are graceful, the windows long. It is evening, moving into night. Birds, mood, stars. It is the pale darkness of mid-September, mild and windless.

On each side of the verandah sits an ageing woman: FLORA, *gently rocking, lost in thought, listening to the music in her head and* NELLIE *who is never at rest. She has never learnt to rest. She has a pile of mending to one side of her, to the other the neatly folded and mended sheets, pillowcases, blouses, tablecloths, stockings. She has the accoutrements for mending beside her in a basket, into which she burrows from time to time for buttons or threads, a thimble or a different needle. She is neat and meticulous in all her actions. She wears over her dark clothes a huge white apron that envelopes her. It is old and well-darned, shiny with starch.*

A voice can be heard singing. It is the music in Flora's head.

Vor der caserne, vor dem grossen tor
Steht'ne laterne, und steht die noch davor?
Si wollen wir uns wiedersehen
Bei der laterne woll'n wir stehen.
Wie einst Lili Marlene,
Wie einst Lili Marlene.
[*Flora sighs.*]
Aus dem stille raume, aus der erde grunde
Hebt sicht wie in traume, dein verliebter mund.
Wenn sich die spaten Nebel drehn
Werd ich bei der laterne stehen
[*The sound of the singing begins to fade away.*]
Wie einst Lili Marlene,
Wie einst Lili Marlene.
FLORA: Again. Over and over again.
　　The song and then the child crying.
　　I hate to hear that child crying.
　　And when the child stops ... I do have to say that, she always

stops ... the world is silent again. Except, of course, for the birds and sometimes the hoover. Nellie hoovers a lot.

That's not a complaint, just a comment.

I often wonder if I am the only person left in the world to remember that song.

A foolish thought, really. The world is full of people who have nothing to do with their lives but remember.

[*There is the faint sound of a young girl crying.*]

There you are. What did I tell you?

It's all so predictable.

I hate that ...

I hate the irrevocability of knowing.

I suspect this is my punishment. Like that man who was condemned to push a stone up a hill forever.

I can't remember his name.

Greek.

For eternity.

At least I don't have to face that.

One of the advantages of being mortal, we don't have to face immortality.

Anyway, to get back to the crying, it never lasts very long.

Just long enough to ... to ... sometimes I can't remember words; quite simple words elude, escape. Stir. Yes, that's the word I want ... stir memory.

I call her sometimes.

Child.

I would like to tell her that she has no need to cry on my behalf.

I can do my own crying, I would say to her, but she never answers.

If I knew her name she might answer.

I never liked being called child.

Mother used to do that: come here, child, run along now, child, time for bed child; just as if she couldn't remember my name.

It will be dark soon and then I will go inside. Nellie will call out to me ... close the window behind you because of the bats.

You can't hear bats after the age of forty. That's a well-known scientific fact. I remember hearing their tiny cries in the evenings. I remember seeing them swooping down towards the lights and the running children. We would scream and cover our heads with our hands as we ran.

Summer evenings, here in this garden. And moths too, dizzy for death in the light from candles and torches.

[*The sound of crying fades.*]

We never cried like that. We were the children of privilege. We had no need to cry, or so we were told. A cut knee qualified for tears, a bee sting, a fall from a pony. There was, they said, no other reason for tears.

NELLIE: There now, that's the buttons on your good silk blouse. I've had to replace them all. It's hard to match those little pearl buttons nowadays. Perhaps, if we were in Dublin, I could run in and out of the shops matching, perusing their stock. If you could just pay attention when they fall off, put them in your pocket or wrap them in a little bit of tissue, not just let them go scattering away.

Are you listening to me?

Need I ask?

Might as well talk to the wall when you have that look on your face.

Come back, Miss Flora Dillon, from wherever you've gone.

FLORA: It's all right, Nellie. I'm here. I never travel very far, you know. [*She laughs slightly.*] I have no maps.

NELLIE: I'm packing up now. I can feel the dampness rising.

FLORA: I could sit here for hours yet ...

NELLIE: And catch your death of cold.

FLORA: ... and watch the ghosts gather.

NELLIE: There are no ghosts. You know that well. There's memories, or dreams, perhaps.

FLORA: You're probably right.

You usually are. How lucky I've been all these years to have you to keep me on the strait and narrow path. Think of me without you ... no buttons on my shirts, no order, no ... no ... We know, you and I, that they would have shut me up years ago, put me for my own good in a home for the harmlessly insane. We know that.

NELLIE: Well, whether we do or whether we don't, we're not going down that path this evening. It's been a good day, full of sun and I've got the mending done. Don't you go and spoil it by getting all peculiar.

I'm away now to put on the potatoes. I've a nice piece of young lamb in the oven and I found a few remaining artichokes in the garden this morning.

FLORA: A feast.

NELLIE: I made an apple tart.

FLORA: Where would I be ...

NELLIE: I thought I'd pop down to the cellar and bring up a couple of bottles of *Gruaud la Rose.*

FLORA: ... without you? Is this a celebration of some sort?

NELLIE: Must give the wine time to breathe. I always feel like a thief in the night creeping down to steal the master's wine. What would he say to me at all if he knew?

FLORA: He'd laugh.

[*She throws her head back and laughs in a boisterous fashion.*]

... and port. Bring up a bottle of port too while you're at it. Might as well be hanged for a sheep as a lamb.

[*Nellie goes out with her bundle of mending.*]

If I had my wits about me, I would know what all this feasting is in aid of. She relishes anniversaries; observes each one with panache.

Poor Nellie.

I know all too well where I would be without her. Out there. Beyond my grandfather's trees. Alone. No *Gruaud la Rose.* Oh dear me no.

I am a woman alone.

That was what mother used to say to make us feel bad.

Your father is battling in the desert and I am a woman alone. You have to help me by being very, very good.

She used to say it to visitors also.

Paul is battling in the desert. Then she would give a little laugh. Paul, Father, Daddy.

It was such a brave little laugh; and then someone would take her hand or touch her lightly on the shoulder, or just give a little sigh. It was his second war.

I used to feel quite sorry for him, when I thought of that.

He got the tail-end of the first one. Eighteen, straight from school.

There are pictures of him all round the house, looking so handsome in his uniform.

So ...

He was my dear friend.

He never explained to me though why he felt he had to go and leave us all. Leave poor mother to be a woman alone.

I missed him so much when he went away.

I missed him so much when he never came back.

He had this wonderful hearty laugh. He used to throw his head right back and roar with laughter. Eddie used to do that too. He had that same laugh.

At night, I used to lie in bed and listen and, from time to time, that laugh of his would come running to me all the way up the stairs.

He would lift me in his arms and put his lips to the side of my neck and blow warm air into my skin. I remember shivering with joy when he did that.

You'll ruin that child, Paul, mother would say.

I dreamed that I would marry him when I grew up; all in white like she had been. White lace dipping to the ground at the back and shorter in the front, showing elegant white satin shoes.

Chicken, I will love you forever, he said in my dreams and blew warm air on my neck.

Bye, chicken was what he'd said when he left, we'll meet again some sunny day. Then he threw back his head and laughed. He never even mentioned the possibility of death.

I was not in any way prepared for that.

El Alamein.

We had this map of North Africa on a table in the drawing room, with all those names on it: Tobruk, Mersa Matruh, Hemiemat, Benghazi, El Alamein.

After we got the news, she drew a little black cross by El Alamein in indelible pencil, because she wasn't able at that moment to find her pen. A few days later, she rolled up the map and put it away as if the war didn't exist any more.

We don't need any more of that was what she said.

We learnt about Khartoum at school; about General Gordon and all that sort of thing. I put up my hand and asked if

Khartoum was anywhere near El Alamein.

No, said Miss Ross, Africa is rather a large place you know, Flora, and everyone giggled.

I would like to have told them about him, about the black cross in indelible pencil, but the words stuck in my mouth. Dry words, like biscuit crumbs, stuck to the roof of my mouth.

Maybe it's just as well. Sometimes there are things you should just keep to yourself.

Mother used to play that song on the wind-up gramophone.

Once I asked her, 'What's that song you play every night?'

'Desert Lullaby'? I didn't realise you could hear it all the way up the stairs. It's really called 'Lili Marlene'. Daddy listens to it in the desert.

How do you know?

He writes to me about all those sort of things.

They all listen to it, he says. All our enemies and all our friends, lying out at night under the desert stars. Trying to fall asleep, trying not to think about the next day.

I call it 'The Desert Lullaby'.

That, of course, was before El Alamein.

When I heard the woman's voice drifting up the stairs after that, I used to think of him, lying under the stars, thinking of us, thinking of home.

I would fall asleep thinking of him. It was comfortable to think of us both listening to the same woman singing us to sleep. After we got the news, she never played the record again.

Broke it in pieces probably. That was the sort of thing she used to do, banging the shellac against the edge of a marble mantelpiece, or cracking it under her heel.

She never wore black.

That was considered strange round here.

Eddie and I had black bands sewn onto the sleeves of our good coats.

Respect and sorrow.

That was what the black band meant.

Nellie told me that when I asked her; she bit through the black thread and then she said that, respect and sorrow.

He never liked me in black, I heard mother say one day to someone.

I used to hear people saying a lot of things.

I could hold my breath and become invisible.

You learn a lot that way.

Yes.

I recommend it.

I always wanted to learn a lot of things I could tell Eddie when he came home from school.

I was always so afraid that he would become bored by having no one around but me to play with.

I sang 'The Desert Lullaby' quietly to myself under the bedclothes at night.

Vor der caserne, vor dem grossen tor ...

Eddie said I shouldn't when he heard me one night. It was, he said, the song of the enemy.

Les Salles Bosches, he called them.

The men who killed Daddy.

I didn't see it like that: I had this picture in my head of all those tired men lying under the stars, listening.

Anyway, I had got so used to the sound of it that I couldn't get to sleep without the sound of those words in my ears. So after that, I whisper-sung them to myself. I told nobody.

... steht'ne laterne, und steht die noch davor.

I hadn't the faintest idea what they meant, but they kept Daddy sleeping in my mind, not dead.

I never learnt German at school.

I had to go away to school.

I learnt a modicum of Latin.

I never wanted to leave this place, but she insisted.

A, ab, absque, coram, de ... that sort of thing.

She was too busy being a woman alone and running the place to be able to occupy herself with broadening my horizons.

Arithmetic, algebra, geometry.

You'll meet girls of your own age, she said. Make friends.

The square on the hypotenuse is equal to the sum of the squares on the other two sides.

I remember the words but lack the meaning.

It's what Daddy would have wanted.

The Statutes of Kilkenny.

The Diet of Worms.

The Repeal of the Act of Union.
The Abolition of the Slave Trade.
All in one ear and out the other.
I learnt to dissimulate; to put a brave face on things.
I learnt not to cry.
I learnt to keep secrets.
I learnt to dance.
But not at school.

[*Music starts to play softly* 'Somebody loves me, I don't know who'. *We are in the drawing room. A wind-up gramophone is playing.* EDDIE *and* YOUNG FLORA *are dancing ... He is seventeen and very confident. She is fifteen and unsure of the steps.*]

I was impolitely bundled from school before the time to start ballroom dancing classes. That was in the lower sixth. Every Thursday evening after prep.

Those of us too young to dance could hear the rhythm from the gramophone in the assembly hall as we sat and read our approved books, or, on summer evenings, played tennis in the almost dark.

[YOUNG FLORA *stumbles over Eddie's feet and they stop.*]

EDDIE: You are hopeless. I'm sure it would be easier to teach a bear to dance. It's like this. Watch. Quick, quick and then turn. See?

YOUNG FLORA: It's all very well for you. You've had lessons. Real lessons. Anyway, I have to do it inside out. I have to keep translating.

EDDIE: You just have to concentrate, that's all. Listen to the music and concentrate. Try it on your own. One and ... slow, quick, quick ... oh Lord, Flora, you are such a mutt.

YOUNG FLORA: I bet I could do it if I had a decent teacher. You get so cross.

EDDIE: I do not.

YOUNG FLORA: Yes, you do. You're foul.

EDDIE: Chuck, chuck, chuck, chuck.

YOUNG FLORA: Oh, hahaha. Very witty.

EDDIE: One more try. Come on. Just relax and follow me. One and ...

[*They dance. They even attempt a showy whirl.*]

That's it. Great girl. You'll be a champion yet.

[*The gramophone begins to slow down. Beeeow beeeow. They laugh.*]

YOUNG FLORA: Beeeeow.

> [*She throws herself onto the sofa.* EDDIE *turns off the gramophone and shuts the lid.*]

Oh, Eddie, do we have to stop?

EDDIE: Enough for one evening. Tell you what, though, if you get it right before the end of the hols, I'll take you down to the Roxy one night.

YOUNG FLORA: Don't be silly. She'd never let us go.

EDDIE: She won't know. And what she doesn't know won't hurt her. One Saturday night after everyone's in bed.

YOUNG FLORA: We'll be caught. There'll be ructions.

EDDIE: I've never been caught yet.

YOUNG FLORA: You've been to ...

EDDIE: Yep.

YOUNG FLORA: You're pulling my leg. I don't believe you.

EDDIE: More than once. It's dead easy. I slip out of this window and leave it unlocked. I just go for an hour or so. No one knows. No harm in it.

YOUNG FLORA: Sometimes I can hear the band on a Saturday night. Sometimes, if the air is still. I love those tunes. I lie and listen to them drifting in the window. Oh Eddie, what's it like down there?

EDDIE: It's great. The band's not half bad. All the lads from the farm are there.

YOUNG FLORA: And girls?

EDDIE: From miles round. All dressed to the nines. You'd hardly recognise them. It's all right, silly. They'll never tell. They think it's a great lark. She'll never find out.

YOUNG FLORA: I'd love to go. But ...

EDDIE: No buts. We'll go. That's fixed. We've been in mourning too long. She can shut herself up for the rest of her life if she wishes, but we don't have to live like that.

> [*Young Nellie's voice calling off.*]

YOUNG NELLIE'S VOICE: Miss Flora. It's past your bed time.

YOUNG FLORA: It's Nellie.

EDDIE: Sssh. Don't say a word. She won't look in here.

YOUNG FLORA: No. I'd better go.

NELLIE'S VOICE: Miss. Missie Flora ...

EDDIE: All that Glen Miller stuff.

[*He begins to hum* 'In The Mood' *and conducts* á la *Glen Miller.*]

NELLIE'S VOICE: I'm not playing hide-and-seek.

YOUNG FLORA: I'm coming. Coooming.

[*She runs to* EDDIE *and kisses him. With one arm he pulls her to him and rubs his face in her hair. He continues to conduct with the other hand. She runs out.*]

EDDIE: 'Mr. whatchacallim what ya doing tonight ... bah
Hope you're in the mood because I'm feeling all right ... bah'.
[*The lights change. We are again on the verandah and* NELLIE *bustles out of the window.*]

NELLIE: Time to come in. Did you nod off?

FLORA: No. I was ...

NELLIE: I called.

FLORA: 'Tell them I called and no one answered ...'

NELLIE: Twice.

FLORA: '... That I kept my word, he said ...'

NELLIE: It's getting cold. Come in now, out of the chill.

FLORA: I'm not cold. It's nice here. It's so quiet out here, I can hear the grass growing.

NELLIE: Will you come in when you're told and don't be asking for trouble. Coughs, chest pains, arthritis, rheumatism. Remember what the doctor said about hospital next time. Come in. Have a bit of sense.

[*She goes back into the room.*]

And close the window behind you because of the bats.

[FLORA *laughs but gets up stiffly and moves indoors. The room is lit by lamps on tables.* NELLIE *is uncorking a wine bottle.*]

FLORA: You know Nellie, bats have a most sophisticated radar system. I really don't think they'll come in here and bother us. I saw a programme about them on television not long ago. They seem quite charming little creatures.

NELLIE: Just close the window and don't be talking such nonsense. Will I put a match tò the fire?

FLORA: No need, the room is still warm from the sun. Did you get the paper?

NELLIE: I forgot. [FLORA *laughs.*] I forgot. I can't remember everything. Dermot Brady called out to me about the nice piece of lamb he'd put aside for us and then I slipped into the church for a few minutes. I forgot.

FLORA: It doesn't matter any more, you know. I have just got so many people to commemorate, so many days and dates. You can't hide them all from me. Pour me a glass of wine and let's work out who we have to drink to today.

NELLIE: It needs to breathe a while. You have no sense at all when it comes to wine. You drink this in the same way you'd knock back the stuff out of the Spar.

FLORA: Pour Nellie. Never mind the breathing. Are we becoming a pair of old winos? Isn't that what they call them nowadays?

NELLIE: There's not too many winos get their hands on this sort of stuff. I can't pronounce the names on all the bottles, but I know the difference between this and Mundies tonic wine. I prefer to be called a conisurio.

[FLORA *laughs. The laugh is echoed by* YOUNG FLORA. *The lights go down. The room is shadowy.* YOUNG FLORA *runs in.* EDDIE *moves out to meet her from the shadows, she is dressed in her best blue silk party dress, white socks to her knees and shiny patent leather shoes.*]

YOUNG FLORA: Here I am. I'm so excited. Is this a terrible thing to be doing? What will happen if mother finds out? Oh golly, Eddie, I dread to think.

EDDIE: How many times do I have to tell you? She's upstairs. She never comes out of her room at this time of night. Anyway, what if she does find out? Where's the harm? There's no harm in dancing. No harm in meeting a few people. If she wants to lock herself up ... mourn forever, that's her affair. She can't expect us to do it too. We have to get on, you know. I'm seventeen after all. Next year I'll be able to leave school and join up ...

YOUNG FLORA: You wouldn't do that ... Eddie. Eddie ...

EDDIE: I certainly would, if I felt like it. No one could stop me. But I'm talking about now. She'll have to raise the blinds one day. Why not now? I'm sick and tired of all this ...

YOUNG FLORA: She says when the war is over. I heard her say that to Aunt Nancy. She says she is in mourning for the whole world. She didn't know I was listening.

EDDIE: Damn silly thing to say. Anyway, whether she is or she isn't, we don't have to be.

YOUNG FLORA: I miss him too. All the time ...

EDDIE: Silly thing. So do I. But our life doesn't have to come to an end. He wouldn't have wanted us to sit here, year after year. He really wouldn't, Flo—believe that.

YOUNG FLORA: In India they fling widows on the funeral pyres of their husbands.

EDDIE: Not sons and daughters. Anyway this is Ireland, 1943, and there isn't a funeral pyre in sight. Come on. Let's get out of here. We're missing the fun.

[*He opens the window and the sound of a distant dance band can be heard.*]

Listen to that. No more hiverhavering. Come on.

[*He holds out his hand to her.*]

YOUNG FLORA: Do I look alright?

EDDIE: You're fine.

[*He laughs.*]

You'll be the prettiest girl there. Give me your hand. I bet you'll dance better than any of them, too. Come on. Let's scoot.

[*As they scoot out through the window into the garden* YOUNG NELLIE *comes from the shadows and watches them across the grass. She remains there staring out as the light comes up on the two women, glasses in hand.*

FLORA *raises her glass to* NELLIE.]

FLORA: To Nellie Maher, friend and conisurio.

NELLIE: Get away with you. Don't go slurping it back like that or you'll be drunk before I have your dinner ready.

FLORA: I think we'll drink to Eddie tonight. I feel him here with us, don't you?

NELLIE: No. No, no, no. I don't feel him here. I don't feel anyone here, only the two of us. You and me. Two old winos.

FLORA: She is here.

NELLIE: She is the cat's mother.

FLORA: By the window. Watching. Over there. Maybe you'll say it's the drink in me seeing things.

NELLIE: And maybe I'd be right.

FLORA: Quite clearly, Nellie. Standing over there. Watching. You were always watching. Weren't you? I never realised at the time. I suppose I was too young to notice such things. He knew though. He remarked on it.

NELLIE: He?

FLORA: Eddie. [*She laughs slightly.*] He said you were a snooper.

NELLIE: Oh no. He shouldn't have said that about me.

FLORA: I thought at the time it was just his joke.

NELLIE: It wasn't like that. It wasn't snooping.

FLORA: But looking back ... maybe it was true.

NELLIE: No. As true as I'm sitting here. It was just ... What's the point in raking up the past. It gets you nowhere.

[YOUNG NELLIE *turns from the window. She holds the blue silk dress in her hand. She walks towards the sofa where* YOUNG FLORA *is sitting, reading.*]

YOUNG NELLIE: Head in a book as usual.

YOUNG FLORA: Mother always says how important it is to be well educated. That's why she decided I had to go away to school.

YOUNG NELLIE: She's right. Otherwise you might end up like me, mending other people's dresses.

YOUNG FLORA: I ...

YOUNG NELLIE: How did it happen?

YOUNG FLORA: We have to wear those dresses every Sunday afternoon at school.

YOUNG NELLIE: Don't tell me lies.

YOUNG FLORA: That's not a lie.

YOUNG NELLIE: It's what my teacher used to call a side-step. Don't you go side-stepping me.

YOUNG FLORA: I must have caught it on a nail or something.

YOUNG NELLIE: Or what?

YOUNG FLORA: I don't remember. I don't have to tell you anything. I haven't done anything wrong.

[NELLIE *stares at her in silence.*]

Nothing wrong.

Don't stare at me like that.

Who do you think you are anyway?

[*She picks up her book again and pretends to read.*]

YOUNG NELLIE: I could go on and on till I got it out of you. I could take it to her and say look at this. Look what she's done to her good school dress. Nearly ripped the sleeve out of it ... and it smells of cigarette smoke. Now, where ...?

YOUNG FLORA: Nellie ...

YOUNG NELLIE: But I won't this time. I'll mend your dress and I'll say nothing.

YOUNG FLORA: There's nothing to say.

YOUNG NELLIE: Don't count on it next time though. My silence. I
go to the pictures on my night off. Thursday. Every Thursday
I go to the pictures. Down and back on the bike. Would you
like to come with me next Thursday? It's *For Me and My Gal.*
Judy Garland. You'd like it. *The bells are ringing for me and my gal.*
The birds are singing for me and my gal, everybody's been knowing to
a wedding they're going and for weeks they've been ...

YOUNG FLORA: You've seen it?

YOUNG NELLIE: Twice and I'm going again on Thursday. What do
you say?

YOUNG FLORA: Do you think she'd let me go?

YOUNG NELLIE: You never know till you try.

YOUNG FLORA: I think I know.

YOUNG NELLIE: I'll get her when she's in a good mood. You never
know your luck. It's a great way of passing the time.

No. It's a great way of living all those lives. Sometimes they're
in colour. We come in from the world and sit there in the dark
and there they live their lives in bright sunny colour. Even
when its black-and-white you believe it's in colour. At least I do.
I become part of their stories. I am in the room watching them.
I feel I only have to stretch out my hand to touch them. Their
lives are real. They are real. Spencer Tracy, Bette Davis,
Humphrey Bogart, James Cagney.

[*She laughs.*]

I read in a book that he's a midget. He has to stand on a box
to do his acting. I don't think I believe that. He doesn't seem
like a man standing on a box to me. Judy Garland and that man
who dances. Fred something. Fred. I'll forget my own name
next. Thursdays. That's the day. She might let you go. There's
no harm in it. I could choose. I would choose very carefully. I
will say that to her.

Last week, oh Flora, it was the most beautiful picture called
Now Voyager. Bette Davis started off as this ugly little runt of a girl
and she had this terrible cross old mother who won't let her do
anything at all, like buy her own clothes or go to parties, but
anyway, and I can't tell you it all because it would take too long,
she ends up with all these lovely men in love with her and
another little girl who she minds and she says to this gorgeous
man in the end. 'We have the moon, why do we want the stars

as well' or something like that. I nearly fell off the bike crying on the way home. It was lovely.

YOUNG FLORA: I don't want to cry. I hate crying. I hate ...

YOUNG NELLIE: This is different. This is gorgeous crying. It's someone else's story and you're crying for them. That makes it different.

YOUNG FLORA: He is going tomorrow. Back to school.

YOUNG NELLIE: They stood there, looking out of this window, and she said that.

YOUNG FLORA: Eddie. Back to ...

YOUNG NELLIE: I often wonder do people say things like that in real life.

YOUNG FLORA: Like what?

YOUNG NELLIE: Like I told you ... about them having the moon and not needing the stars as well.

YOUNG FLORA: I don't suppose they do.

They seem to stick to more everyday sort of things.

Bye chicken. We'll meet again some sunny day.

I am a woman alone.

People say things like that.

And no. They say no. Always no, it seems to me.

YOUNG NELLIE: For your own good.

It's lucky Master Eddie's off tomorrow, so there'll be no more slipping out at night and making a show of yourself. There's not too many people round here keep their lips buttoned. You can thank your lucky stars she didn't get to hear of what you done. I'll mend your dress and she'll never know and I'll ask her about the pictures, but you'll have to behave yourself in future.

YOUNG FLORA: I don't believe I have any lucky stars.

YOUNG NELLIE: Bette Davis, Deanna Durbin, Judy Garland. They can be your stars. Tell you what we'll do and we coming back from the pictures, we'll name the stars. Spencer Tracy, Cary Grant ... they'll look after you then, named magic stars ... Mickey Rooney ...

[*As* NELLIE *takes over, the two young girls disappear.*]

NELLIE: God, I haven't thought about Mickey Rooney in years. Another little runt of a fellow. We never did that, did we?

FLORA: She said no.

NELLIE: I'm sure she had her reasons.

FLORA: I used to wonder if she'd have said no if father hadn't been killed. You're probably right. She had my best interests at heart.

If father hadn't been killed I would have had freedom, friends, the stars to look after me, father to look after me. And Eddie. I'm sure Eddie wouldn't have gone if ... if ... if ... if ... Damn ifs.

I'm sure she felt I should want to live in mourning as she did.

Yes, I'll have another glass of wine.

For how long, I asked her once.

Until this dreadful war is over, she shouted at me.

You weren't there when she shouted those words at me.

You must have been at the pictures.

Yes.

Thank you.

It must have been that same autumn and I was going back to school. We were on the station platform and she shouted those words at me.

I remember the sound of the train whistle streaming across the fields and I felt happy to be going away.

I felt pleasure at the thought of leaving the sad prison that my home had become.

I cried because I was glad to be going away. She didn't cry. She stood on the platform and stared into the past.

She didn't even wave at me as we chugged away. Didn't look or smile. Nothing.

NELLIE: Don't get yourself all worked up. I don't want to have to call the doctor over in the middle of the night

FLORA: I used to dream about father.

Did you know that?

Out there in the desert under the stars.

It was cold.

Did you know, Nellie, that it was cold in the desert?

I learnt that at school.

It was odd. I could feel that cold and I always heard that woman singing and he was walking towards me and all the time the sand shifted under his feet.

She sang.

Wie einst Lili Marlene.

And he was trying so hard to get home.

Wie einst Lili Marlene.

Each step he took towards me, the sand shifted more under his feet.

The sand wouldn't let him move.

He wasn't in uniform.

I never saw him in his uniform, you know. Only all those pictures of him young and handsome.

His first war.

Through the woman's voice I could hear the big guns and one night I called out ... Daddy, here. This way. I am waiting for you. Here.

Then I woke up and found Eddie in his pyjamas standing by my bed and the cold desert stars shining through the window. I heard you calling me—he said and I said—No, I was calling Daddy. I want him to come home ...

NELLIE: I never knew ...

FLORA: He won't, Eddie said. He can't. You know that. You'll have to put up with me instead.

He put out his hand and began to stroke my hair and the sound of the guns faded slowly and the sound of the woman singing and I fell asleep.

I can remember even now the feel of his fingers stroking my hair, and you never knew that?

NELLIE: No.

FLORA: There was a time when I thought you knew everything.

NELLIE: It ...

FLORA: But you didn't. No one knows everything.

NELLIE: ... was my job. Keep an eye on the ...

FLORA: You never knew, for instance ...

NELLIE: ... child. That was what she said. Keep an eye ...

FLORA: ... why she sent me away like that.

Year upon year, shut up in that place.

The harmlessly insane. God, I heard those words repeated so many times.

It's all for your own good.

You're safe here. That's what they kept saying.

You never knew what that was like.

NELLIE: They were good to you. They were never unkind.
It was for your own good.

[FLORA *laughs.*]

FLORA: Oh Nellie... You always believed them, didn't you? All those
ridiculous things they said. Those distorted sentences ... and
mother, you believed her too. If anyone was mad it was mother.
I suppose she was driven mad by grief ...
Distorted.
Such distorted lives we lead because of our own folly.
I often wonder why she hated me so much.
I didn't kill my father, or Eddie.
It was history killed them.
'Paths of glory' ...
I don't suppose there was much glory really, in spite of what
the poets all say.
Father felt it was his duty to go and poor old Eddie really
didn't have much time to think about it at all.

[*The faint sound of dance music playing. It is night and the moon
shines into the room.* EDDIE *is standing by the window staring out into
the garden. The gramophone is playing.* NELLIE *moves across the stage
and out through the garden.* EDDIE *watches her as she goes.* YOUNG
FLORA *comes in carrying an oil lamp, which she puts on the table.*]

YOUNG FLORA: Oh, there you are. I was looking for you everywhere
and then I heard the music.

[*As she is speaking he pulls the curtains tightly.*]

Is that Benny Goodman? Why are you pulling the curtains?
It's such a lovely night.

EDDIE: I thought I saw her out there.

YOUNG FLORA: Mother?

EDDIE: No. Don't be an ass. Not mother. What would mother be
doing out in the garden at this time of night? That Nellie girl.
You're quite pally with her, aren't you?

YOUNG FLORA: She's nice. She was going to take me to the pictures
last holidays after you'd gone back to school, but mother
wouldn't let me go.

EDDIE: I think she's a bit of a snooper.

YOUNG FLORA: Of course she's not. What a horrid thing to say.

EDDIE: I get the feeling she's following me around. Everywhere I
go she seems to be there, staring at me.

YOUNG FLORA: Perhaps she's ... *amoureuse de toi...* that's what the girls at school say ... *je suis un peu amoureuse de lui* ... silly, isn't it? But it sounds so romantic. *Am ... our ... euse.* Are we going down to the Roxy? I must go and put on my dress if we are.

EDDIE: No.

YOUNG FLORA: What a shame. I was really hoping we might go. There are so few days left before we go back to school. I've been practising ... I've really improved. You must admit I don't stand on your toes any more. [EDDIE *crosses the room and turns off the gramophone.*] What's the matter? You've been grumpy all day. Have you had a row with her?

EDDIE: I'm not going back to school.

YOUNG FLORA: What! You're not ... does she know? What are you going to do? Oh Eddie, are you going to stay here? If she's going to let you stay at home, please get her to let me too. Please, please. Is she going to let you work on the farm?

Oh, golly, don't tell me she's going to stop being a woman alone. But what ... Eddie ... tell me ...

EDDIE: Will you stop? You'll have the whole house in here if you go on making such a racket. Sit down, Flora, for heaven's sake and stop capering around.

YOUNG FLORA: Tell me, tell me ...

EDDIE: Sit down. I'm trying to tell you. I've been wanting to tell you all hols, but I promised not to. Here. Down. By me.

YOUNG FLORA: Promised not to tell me. Who? Why? You never have secrets from me. Eddie... who?

EDDIE: Calm down. I promised Wilkinson not to tell. We swore just to keep it tight inside ourselves. I shouldn't even be telling you now. But I trust you. Honestly, I really trust you.

YOUNG FLORA: Who is Wilkinson?

EDDIE: He is my friend.

YOUNG FLORA: You've never mentioned him to me.

EDDIE: Why should I? What can I say to you about Wilkinson, Baggot, Evans, Baillie? What would they mean to you? You don't know what they look like. You don't know the sounds of their voices. I might just as well tell you fairy tales. They don't belong in this life. Nor do I any more. This is a prison we live in here.

YOUNG FLORA: Wilkinson, Baggot, Evans, Baillie.

EDDIE: My friends. We mess around together. Talk, you know. Wilkinson and I are ... well, his father's gone too, you know, missing, believed ... we have that sort of... sorrow in common.

YOUNG FLORA: What's his name?

EDDIE: His name?

YOUNG FLORA: He must have a name. Everyone has a name.

EDDIE: His mother calls him Patch ...

YOUNG FLORA: You've met his mother?

EDDIE: But I think his name is Patrick.

YOUNG FLORA: Think?

EDDIE: Patrick. Wilkinson P.H.. He has a younger brother. Wilkinson. R.J.. He calls him Tot. He's new. Only thirteen. A decent kid.

YOUNG FLORA: How silly it all is, not to know people's names.

EDDIE: It's all right you know. We're friends.

YOUNG FLORA: Well?

EDDIE: Well what?

YOUNG FLORA: What about telling me this great secret that you've been hiding for so long. Your Wilkinson secret.

[EDDIE *gets up and crosses the room to the door. He opens it and looks outside, then closes it again.*]

EDDIE: You must promise not to breathe a word to anyone. Swear. [*She crosses her heart and holds out her hand to him.*] We're going to join up. It's all arranged. On Friday I'm getting off the train at Crewe and he's going to meet me there.

YOUNG FLORA: No.

EDDIE: He's been finding out all the know-how ... so we don't make bloody fools of ourselves. I got a letter from him yesterday saying ... Bam! Go ahead. Imagine, in three days, Flora, I'll be in the war.

YOUNG FLORA: No.

EDDIE: Yes. Yes I will. This is going to be the ...

YOUNG FLORA: No. No. No. You can't do this. You're too young. They won't let you. You can't. You ...

EDDIE: We can, you know. I'm nearly eighteen. I could have joined up at the end of last term but we wanted to get it all organised. We're going to the depot at Crewe and ...

[YOUNG FLORA *starts to run to the door, but he catches her before she reaches it.*]

Where do you think you're going?

YOUNG FLORA: To tell mother. You're such a fool, Eddie. She won't let you go. You're still at school. You're hurting my arm. Let go of me. You can't do this. You can't leave us. You ...

EDDIE: Stop making all that racket. You'll have the snooper in. Come on. Come on, sit down here and let's talk. You promised. You know you can't break a promise. Here, wipe your face. Blow your nose. You're behaving like a baby. Can't you shut up... oh God Flora, why did I tell you? Wilkinson will kill me. Don't cry. I'll be O.K. Come on, cheer up.

YOUNG FLORA: You'll be killed.

EDDIE: Of course I won't be killed.

YOUNG FLORA: Daddy was killed.

EDDIE: That's no reason why I should be. He would have wanted me to go.

YOUNG FLORA: No, he wouldn't. You're still at school. He would have wanted ...

EDDIE: You're too young to know anything about it. I only told you because I thought you would think it was a lark. I didn't want to go away without you knowing. I didn't want you to think that I was deceiving you in some way. And now look ... you're behaving like a baby.

YOUNG FLORA: I am not.

EDDIE: You're spoiling everything. Like a baby.

YOUNG FLORA: Oh, Eddie.

[*He pulls her into his arms and kisses her face. He dabs at her tears with his handkerchief.*]

EDDIE: Don't cry. Please. Don't make me feel rotten. Please. Smile. Just a little smile. Please. I'll miss you too. Only you. I hate this life here ... and there's father.

YOUNG FLORA: What about father?

EDDIE: No matter what you think, he would have wanted me to go. Step into his shoes, if you like. I know. I really do know that.

YOUNG FLORA: No. I can only say no. And go on and on saying no.

EDDIE: It doesn't matter what you say. It's all arranged. I can't back out now, even if I wanted to. I have promised ... You must promise, too. Please Flora. Secret. Look, tomorrow night we'll dance. Here. Just you and me. Dressed up to the nines. My last night at home. Give me something to remember. Hey? Here.

I'll pick out all the best records and we'll ... What do you say?

YOUNG FLORA: I don't know. It's a bit like a seal of approval, isn't it?

EDDIE: No. I won't think of it like that. It will be a ball. Our ball. Like the night before Waterloo. Here, with the curtains tight pulled, so the snooper can't see in, and candles. We'll have candles. We can dance all night until our feet give up. And I will go on the morning train and no one will know. Please say yes. Please, Flora.

YOUNG FLORA: You always win, don't you?

EDDIE: There's a great girl.

[*He hugs her and blows gently on the side of her neck. She cries out and pushes him away.*]

What's the matter?

YOUNG FLORA: Don't do that. I can't bear it when you do that. Yes. We'll do it. Late tomorrow night. No one. Just you and I.

EDDIE: And you won't say a word?

[YOUNG FLORA *shakes her head. Nellie's voice is heard calling.*]

NELLIE: Dinner's ready.

[*She comes onto the stage.*]

We mustn't let it spoil.

FLORA: You knew, didn't you?

NELLIE: I knew everything. I was always there.

FLORA: Why didn't you stop it?

NELLIE: Sure, where was the harm? A bit of dressing up, a bit of dancing. No harm at all. Anyway, wasn't it Thursday? I was at the pictures. Come and have your dinner. Let me take your arm. The wine makes you totter a bit.

[*They cross the stage arm in arm and the lights go down.*]

[*End of Act One.*]

ACT TWO

The room is dim, lit only by candles and the light from a flickering fire. On one table is a bottle of champagne and two beautiful Venetian glasses.

The curtains are tightly pulled.

EDDIE, *dressed in his father's officer's uniform, Irish Guards, World War I, is winding up the gramophone. Carefully, he puts on a record and lowers the needle onto it. It is Glen Miller. He stands listening for a moment and then with a childish grin on his face he begins to conduct. His back is to the gramophone, as if it were the orchestra.*

FLORA *and* NELLIE *come in.* FLORA *carries a glass in her hand and* NELLIE *also has the bottle. They cross the room to the fireplace.* NELLIE *puts the bottle on a table.*

FLORA: No. Don't turn on the light. [*She sits down in her armchair in the shadows.*] They'll go away if you turn on the light.

NELLIE: How can I see without the light? I have the paper to read. We have to pick our horses for tomorrow. I have to digest the odds, the correspondents' little tips. I can't do that in the dark, can I? How many times have I told you that there's nothing here to see. You and me, that's all.

FLORA: Sssh. This was when she came in. I remember the music so well. Just at that moment ...

[*The door opens and* YOUNG FLORA *stands in the light from the passageway outside. She is dressed in one of her mother's evening dresses, high-heel shoes, her face made up, her hair piled up on her head. She looks wonderful, almost in fact unrecognisable.*]

... Aaaah.

[*As she speaks,* EDDIE *turns round and sees* YOUNG FLORA *in the doorway. He thinks for a moment it is his mother. He is confused. He stops conducting. Stands like a child caught out.*]

EDDIE: I ... ah ... mother ... [*Both Floras laugh, throwing back their heads.*] ... Flora!

YOUNG FLORA: I fooled you. Didn't I fool you? What do you think? Don't I look like a dream?

[*She begins to dance around the room. He watches her, almost entranced.*]

EDDIE: You fooled me. Just for a moment. One moment. That's all. I thought you were ...

YOUNG FLORA: Yes. Yes. Yes. Nellie was out at the pictures and I crept into the dressing-room and there were all these wonderful, butterfly clothes, shawls, dresses, velvet, silk, shawls, veils, cloaks. How beautiful she must have looked then. How ...

EDDIE: Yes. Like you. Just like you.

[*The music slows down ... eeeow eeeoww and she swirls slower and slower with it. The music stops. For the first time she takes in the uniform he is wearing.*]

YOUNG FLORA: That's Daddy's uniform you're ...

EDDIE: Yes. I thought I would surprise you. Instead you have surprised me.

YOUNG FLORA: ... Perhaps you shouldn't have ...

EDDIE: It smells of moth balls. Rather disgusting.

[*They stand for a moment, staring at each other.* EDDIE *breaks first. He laughs nervously.*]

I went down to the cellar and got some ...

[*He indicates the champagne.*]

YOUNG FLORA [*putting on a posh voice*]: Champagne. Darling, how too, too marvellous. [*They both lapse into childishness again.*]

You pinched it and their Venetian glasses. Gosh. What an evening of sin. I bet you can't open it without it fizzing all over the place.

EDDIE: I can. Wilkinson showed me how.

YOUNG FLORA: Wilkinson again!

EDDIE: You take off the wire ... so ... and then ... you keep your hand over the cork, like this and edge it ... Glass, get a glass quickly it's coming.

[*The cork pops out and* FLORA *catches the wine in a glass.* NELLIE *folds up her newspaper and stares at the two young people as they fill their glasses.*]

NELLIE: That was the Master's *Veuve Clicquot.* I remember the day that arrived. It was just before he left for the war and he said it wasn't to be touched until the war was over. My victory champagne, he said it was ... There's a couple of bottles of it below still.

FLORA: Ssssh.

YOUNG FLORA: Did you hear something?

EDDIE: Don't be silly. Everyone's in bed. A toast. We have to drink a toast. Our wonderful future.

[*They touch glasses.*]

YOUNG FLORA: Our wonderful future. [*They drink.*]
Oooh, how I love this. I'll drink nothing but champagne when I grow up.

[*He splashes more into their glasses.*]

EDDIE: There's plenty more where that came from.
You look so beautiful drinking champagne.

[*She throws her head back and laughs.*]

FLORA: Yes. That was such a happy moment.

NELLIE: Scamps.

EDDIE: Don't laugh, I mean it.

YOUNG FLORA: I'm happy. This is what happiness is. I've often wondered. You read the word in books and wonder about it. Now I know. Thank you, Eddie.

[*She throws her arms around him and hugs him and manages to spill champagne on his clothes.*]

EDDIE: Hey!

YOUNG FLORA: Oh, I'm so sorry. Here ... let me ...

EDDIE: It doesn't matter. It really doesn't ... who'll ever know anyway? I'll put it all back in the tin trunk and no one will ever take it out again. Come on, fill up. We must dance. We have so little time left.

[*He winds up the gramophone and takes a second record from the pile and puts it on the turntable. She takes a large gulp and sneezes.*]

YOUNG FLORA: Oh, bless my soul.

EDDIE: Bless you.

[*He puts the needle on the turntable. 'A Nightingale Sang in Berkeley Square.' He drains his glass and holds out a hand to her. She drains her glass and moves towards him. He takes her hand and kisses it and they begin to dance.*]

FLORA: I think we should have some champagne too. Don't you, Nellie?

NELLIE: There's only a couple of bottles left.

FLORA: So?

NELLIE: Haven't you had enough for one evening?

FLORA: This isn't any old evening.

NELLIE: We should keep them till we win the Derby. That's the time for champagne. That's the time for being flahoola.

FLORA: If we win the Derby, I promise you we'll buy some more. Replenish the Master's cellar. After all, Nellie, we can't take it with us. If you don't want to go down to the cellar, I'll go—I'll make the adventurous descent.

NELLIE: And fall and break your neck. You'll do no such thing. Dr ...

FLORA: Don't Nellie. No threats of doctors tonight. If I suffer tomorrow from a hangover, that will be my own affair. Will you go or will I go?

NELLIE: You sound just like your mother when you carry on like that.

FLORA: I do hope not. Well?

NELLIE: I'll go. But don't say ...

FLORA: Not a word. I won't say a word. I will carry my hangover with grace and silently.

NELLIE: Hmmpphh.

[*She gets up and heads across the room, past the dancers as if they were not there.* FLORA *smiles as she watches her go.*]

FLORA: He left the next morning.

The trap came for him when it was barely light.

[*As she talks the two young people stop dancing. They fill their glasses and* EDDIE *winds the gramophone.* 'These Foolish Things.' *They dance again, slow and close together.*]

I was woken by the clopping of the pony's hooves.

Otherwise I might not have seen him go.

'Season of mists'. That was right. They melted into that mist.

I stood just inside the window and looked down at them.

Mother on the steps wrapped warm in a big shawl.

I was afraid to go down. I was afraid he might frown at me, perhaps be displeased with me.

And Nellie stood, holding his attaché case in her hand, as he said his goodbyes to mother.

It all looked so normal.

He wore his grey flannel school suit.

See you at Christmas, darling ... I imagined mother saying that as she touched his face.

She wasn't really a kisser.

The floor beneath my feet was cold.

It was all so normal.

I wanted to throw the window open and shout. 'He's going to the war with Wilkinson.'

How I hated promises at that moment.

'Season of mists'.

He got into the trap, looking like a schoolboy and Nellie handed him his case. Toothbrush, hairbrush, flannel, pyjamas, clean socks, pack of cards. We had packed it the day before.

Always a pack of cards for long boat or train journeys.

Yes.

He got into the trap, his knees touching the boy's knees and leant out to say goodbye to Nellie.

Even from my bedroom window, I could see that she was crying. He held her hand for a moment and said something to her.

Some lie like: See you soon. I'll be back in a jiffy. One of those sort of short meaningless sentences.

As he slammed the trap door, and as the boy shook the reins over the pony's back, he looked up towards my window and I stepped back so that he wouldn't see me, not even the whiteness of my nightdress glimmering, in the darkness of the window.

He looked like a schoolboy.

[*The music ends and they stand very close to each other. The turntable clicks round and round.*]

YOUNG FLORA: What fun they must have had. All that dancing in the days of their youth.

EDDIE: We have it all in front of us. Just think what fun we will have. How beautiful you will be. I will be quite jealous of all your lovers.

[*With a little laugh she breaks away from him and empties the bottle into her glass.*]

YOUNG FLORA: Lovers! It's difficult to think of lovers when your head is full of French irregular verbs and Archimedes' Principle. 'I wandered lonely as a cloud, that floats on high o'er ...'

EDDIE: You'll forget all that. You'll forget this evening.

YOUNG FLORA: Oh, no. No, Eddie, how could I ever forget this evening? The trouble with champagne seems to be that it disappears too quickly.

EDDIE: Abracadabra. Hey Presto.

[*He produces another bottle as if by magic. She claps her hands and he opens it. They fill their glasses.* NELLIE *comes across the room with a bottle cradled in her arms like a baby.*]

NELLIE: There you are. Two more left. Two more celebrations that means. Two Derbys, perhaps. The Grand National. What about the Prix de L'Arc de Triomphe? That'd be something to celebrate, wouldn't it?

FLORA: Give it to me. I'll open it.

NELLIE: Your fingers will never manage.

FLORA: Of course they'll manage. You get the glasses. The good ones. The beautiful Venetian glasses. Just the thing.

[*She begins to fumble with the bottle.* NELLIE *crosses the room and opens a cupboard. She takes out one glass and holds it up to the light and then polishes it with her apron, then another.* EDDIE *is winding up the gramophone again and* YOUNG FLORA *is looking through the records.*]

YOUNG FLORA: Oh!

[*She holds up a record towards* EDDIE.]

Where did you get this? I thought she had ...

EDDIE: What's that?

[*As he takes the record and looks at it,* NELLIE *comes back across the room holding the two glasses out in front of her.*]

Oh, that. Wilkinson gave me that last term. Do you want me to put it on?

[*The champagne pops and* FLORA *fills the glasses.*]

FLORA: I told you I could do it.

YOUNG FLORA: I don't know.

FLORA: They bought them on their honeymoon in Venice. He told me that.

EDDIE: Why not?

YOUNG FLORA: Why not?

FLORA: Here's to us, Nellie. Survivors.

[EDDIE *and* YOUNG FLORA *clink glasses and then he puts the record on.*]

What's the point in surviving? I often wonder that. All the trouble they go to to make sure you survive.

Vor der caserne, vor dem grossen tor
Steht'ne laterne, und steht die noch davor ...

[*The gramophone joins in with her and the two young people begin to dance slowly and very close together.*]

NELLIE: War songs. Why do you sing war songs? You've had too much to drink. Your mind is kindling up. I know the symptoms. I know ...

FLORA: Nothing. He was wrong when he called you a snooper. He should have known better than that. You were too good, too kind to have the need to spy. It wouldn't have entered your head. Come and sit here beside me and I'll tell you something you never knew.

Why?

I see why in your face.

I know what day it is.

Fifty years ago he left us. You and me.

I used to blame Wilkinson for everything. Poor Wilkinson, how upset he would have been if he'd known that I blamed him for Eddie's death [*She laughs.*]

The absurdity of blaming people.

I felt I had to blame someone. I used to beat the wall with my fists and scream. Bang my head, bruise my face. I wanted to kill myself but they wouldn't let me. That always seemed so unfair. They strapped me to my bed when I became wild. They gave me drugs that made my tongue swell in my mouth so that I couldn't speak out the words I wanted to say.

It is for your own good.

You say they were kind.

It is for your own good.

I only wanted to die. For my own good.

NELLIE: You're talking about sin. They couldn't let you commit a sin like that. Think of God. The good God. Think of never seeing his face. It's the drink in you talking. They were right. You wouldn't be here now if it hadn't been for those good people.

FLORA: I can't say I'd mind very much. Don't get me wrong, Nellie.

I have a great love for you—I would have missed that in my life.

I would have been the poorer dying before I knew that love.

NELLIE: Get away with you.

FLORA: You could have had a real life.

YOUNG FLORA: 'The Desert Lullaby'.

EDDIE: Why do you say that?

YOUNG FLORA: That's what he used to call it.

[*The song comes to an end and they stand holding each other. He bends his head and gently blows against the side of her neck. She gasps and staggers slightly. He holds her tighter.*]

FLORA: No. No, please ...

EDDIE: Sssh ... Let me kiss you, Flora. Really kiss you.

YOUNG FLORA: I don't ...

[*She tries to push him away.*]

EDDIE: Just a kiss. You wouldn't let me go away without a kiss. You couldn't be so cruel. Just a ...

YOUNG FLORA: Cruel? How can you say cruel?

EDDIE: She'd kiss me. I know that, I can see it in her face. Everytime I look at her, I can see what she's thinking.

YOUNG FLORA: She?

EDDIE: The spy.

[FLORA *begins to laugh.*]

NELLIE: I don't think he should have said that. That wasn't very kind. Did you think that was kind?

FLORA: I don't remember what I thought I ...

NELLIE: You laughed.

[EDDIE *begins to kiss her laughing face and she throws her arms around his neck and kisses him back.*]

FLORA: ... don't remember. I don't remember who I was or who he was. I thought nothing at that time. It was her dress, her scent, her beauty and he was Daddy. It was all right.

NELLIE: It was not all right. And had I known what the pair of you were up to, I'd a been in there double quick and put a stop to it. It was the drink.

FLORA: Probably. Loneliness. Fear. Sorrow. Perhaps even love but, as I say, I don't remember.

[*As they have been talking, the young pair move slowly off-stage. The lights on them dim.*]

Fill up the glasses, Nellie. No point in leaving champagne in the bottle.

You could have had a life. Do you never regret that?

NELLIE: What have I had? What is this I'm leading? Isn't my belly full of good food and drink? I'm at peace. What more can anyone want? I never had very high expectations, you know.

When I came to work here, I thought I might rise to be the housekeeper. My mother always told me that a housekeeper was a person of power. A person with a dignity of their own. That's what I had in mind. Miss Maher. I had it in mind to be Miss Maher when I walked down to the village and went into the shops. Perhaps I might have had a little motor car so that I could drive myself to the pictures on Thursday evenings. One of those nice little Morrises. Remember them? I could have managed that.

FLORA: Oh, dear Nellie. If only you'd said. I'm sure we could have got you a car. We still could. I'll talk to Mr. ...

NELLIE: Don't worry your head. You have to have a certificate nowadays to drive a car. I'd never manage that. I've grown accustomed to the bike. I like the old bike.

FLORA: Maybe I could get a bike too.

[NELLIE *laughs.*]

No laughing matter, Nellie. They say that once you know how to ride a bike, you know forever. I seem to remember I used to be very daring. No hands, that sort of thing. I'm sure it would come back to me in no time.

NELLIE: Would you stop your foolishness. Think of the trouble I'd be in if Doctor Carey saw you scooting down the hill to the village with no hands.

FLORA: An absurd sight, I agree, but ...

NELLIE: But me no buts.

FLORA: Shakespeare.

NELLIE: My backside. My mother said it all the time.

FLORA: Shakespeare.

NELLIE: No is the only answer. I promised her. In spite of all the carry on of her down the years, I suppose I loved her. A bit like yourself, I'd no one else to love. So, I promised. She made me put my hand on the Bible and swear that I would mind you here, forever. It's the only place for her, she said, and then perhaps God will forgive me for what I did. She said that.

Whatever she was talking about I never knew. But I had to swear. She said they'd keep you there in that place if I didn't swear.

FLORA: No one should be bound like that.

NELLIE: What do you do when you make a promise before God?

You can't wriggle out of that one. To tell the truth, the notion of minding you, mad and all as she said you were, wasn't near as bad as the notion of going out into the world after all those years. This place had become my home. I'd have found it very hard to go away from here. Frightening. So I promised. I put my hand on the Bible. She put her hand on mine just to make sure. Held it tight. Like this.

[*She holds Flora's hand.*]

Her hand was strong. Even at the end. There was no escaping her.

FLORA: Eddie managed it.

NELLIE: That's not a very nice thing to say.

FLORA: I don't think he ever would have come back you know, if he hadn't been killed. Perhaps just for a fleeting visit. Funerals, family duties. D-Day plus two. That's what they called it. I often wonder, when we look at those old news reels on television, will I see him. I scour those faces to try and catch a sight of him. And then I laugh to myself. Would I recognise him after all those years?

NELLIE: I'd recognise him.

FLORA: Did he drown, weighted down with all that gear? Was he shot by a sniper? Blown up by a German shell? Did he lie wounded for hours on a stony beach?

No one ever told me.

Was he a hero or a coward?

To me he was a silly schoolboy who didn't know what he was fighting for.

Running away.

Did Wilkinson survive?

Did Wilkinson survive?

I often wonder that.

NELLIE: I never heard tell of Wilkinson.

FLORA: In one way, I'd like them to have died side by side, like in the legends, defending each other. You never like to think of someone you love dying amongst strangers.

Tell me something. I've always wanted to know. Would you have kissed him if he'd asked you?

NELLIE: If, if, if. If *ifs* and *ands* were pots and pans ... I suppose you'll tell me now that's Shakespeare, too.

FLORA: Don't be cross with me, Nellie.

NELLIE: And why shouldn't I be cross? Stirring up all this old rubbish. Rubbish. That's all it is. Isn't that why you were shut up like that all those years? Your head was teeming with rubbish.

They had to clean out the inside of your head. Make you come sane again. Stabilise.

That's what she said to me. One day she'll be stabilised and then she can come home again.

You were such a good little girl.

I wanted you to come home and be stabilised.

This place was lonely enough with no young people about.

I never could work out why I stayed.

I suppose I got used to the life.

I couldn't see a place for myself anywhere else, so I stayed on and on and then it was too late to go.

Anyway, she said you'd have to stay in that old place in England if I wasn't here to mind you.

That's what she said, right enough.

Sometimes she said things that weren't quite true.

I asked her once why she didn't bring you home.

That was when she was still well, going about, being a person.

You mind your own business, Nellie. Real cross she was. Don't speak to me about Flora. Ever again. She'll come home when she's well. Not a second before. Understand?

Sometimes I found her quite hard to understand, though I never said as much. She had a hard life, when you come to think of it. I must say I was upset when they closed down the picture house in the village.

I felt I'd lost a lot of friends then.

I tried biking into Wicklow town, but it was too far. I hated that long ride back in the dark.

Anyway, they showed a different sort of picture then.

I liked dreaming pictures, pictures that made you feel there was always hope.

I can be cross.

I have a right to be cross.

You ask me damn silly questions.

FLORA: I'm sorry, Nellie.

NELLIE: You say he called me a spy.

FLORA: He didn't mean it. Not in a bad way.

NELLIE: I couldn't help it. I just wanted to be near him. I wanted to
see him every day, learn about him, know things about him that
I could treasure in my head for ever. Bye Nellie, he said when
I handed him up his case into the trap, we'll meet again some
sunny day.

[FLORA *starts to laugh.*]

　　Go ahead and laugh.

　　I believed him.

　　I could see that sunny day in my head, like in the pictures.
I didn't know he was going to the war. I didn't know he had
such a thought in his head. He was just Master Eddie, off to
school again and he'd be back some sunny day.

　　I'd be there.

　　Yes.

　　The answer is yes. I'd have kissed him.

　　I wish you hadn't asked the question. The answer is yes.

[*The lights come up in the room. It is early morning. The curtains are
still pulled, but a little daylight slips in through them. There is the
sound of a trap driving away. The sound of the hall door closing and
then, after a moment,* YOUNG NELLIE *comes into the room. She crosses the
room and pulls open the curtains. It is a lovely autumn morning. She
stares out after the vanishing trap and when it is no longer in her sight
she looks around the room.*

　　*The bottles, the good Venetian glasses, the open gramophone. She
begins to tidy up and then sees the rumpled dress on the sofa. She picks
it up and looks at it for a moment and then holds it against her. She
begins to hum something like* 'South of the Border, Down Mexico
Way' *and she dances a few swirling steps. She stops humming after a
few moments, overcome with tears and sits down on the sofa, her face
buried in the dress.*

　　NELLIE *gets to her feet.*]

NELLIE: Child ...

[NELLIE *walks over to the weeping girl and lays her hand on her head
for a moment. Then she stoops down and picks up the high-heeled shoes
that are on the floor by the sofa. Gently, she sits and puts them on her
knee.*]

　　Put them away tidily in Madame's press. We wouldn't want

anyone to know that they've been used and take care of them good Venetian glasses.

[*As the lights dim, she leaves the room.*]

FLORA: Now look what I've done.

All this digging up. This reincarnating ...

She'll be all right. I know that. She'll make a cup of tea.

I won't tell her any more.

No.

Some secrets are better left untold.

She'll bring me a cup of tea and then it will all be over.

Maybe I am insane.

Harmlessly, of course.

[*She laughs.*]

Full of untruthful memories.

I mean to say what does 'harmless' mean?

I only ever wanted to harm myself.

I was the only person I ever hated enough to harm.

I was no threat to anyone. I suppose that was what they meant. Except, of course, to her. Mother.

My blabbing tongue.

Better to have a mad daughter unhinged like Ophelia by sorrow than one defiled and disgraced.

I am a woman alone.

She didn't have to be.

Even after they shut me up in England, she was the only person I had to love.

I don't know why I felt I had to love her. Habit? Honour thy father and thy mother ... that sort of thing.

It was the school doctor blew the whistle on me.

The winter term.

I was such an innocent fool.

It never occurred to me what might be wrong with me.

The sky was rock hard.

Nowhere was warm in that last year of the war, even in Dublin. Smoke from turf fires stung your eyes.

I kept my eyes tight shut when he examined me.

His hands were cold.

As I dressed behind a screen, I could hear him washing his hands. I imagined the warm water running over his fingers.

He cleared his throat and then called out to me.

Have you really no idea what the matter might be?

I came out from behind the screen.

Cold.

No.

He stood by the basin, the towel in his hand and looked at me for a long time without saying a word.

I hope it's nothing serious.

Nothing life threatening, he said. You can go now.

I'll speak to the head.

Later, after break, it was Latin class, Miss Murphy who I never liked. Virgil's Aeneid. Book Four.

Facilis descensus Averni; noctes atque dies patet atri ianua Ditis; sed revocare gradum superasque evadere ad auras, hoc opus, hic labor est.

[*She laughs.*]

How truly batty the mind is.

I used to stumble and tremble over those words when I needed them and now they dance off my tongue as if they had lived forever in the front of my mind.

The head came for me herself and took me to her room without saying a word.

I don't know what you've been up to, young lady, but you're pregnant.

I shook my head.

No was all I could say.

I couldn't understand.

Yes. I have informed your mother and she is coming up on the next train. Your case is being packed and you are not to leave this room until she comes for you.

But how could I be ...?

I began to cry.

How could I be ...?

She wasn't too bad, really.

She gave me a handkerchief and sat me down. She called for tea and from time to time patted my shoulder. I think she was afraid for herself, her reputation, her school.

I couldn't speak. I could only shake my head and cry.

She had to get me another handkerchief.

Even after my mother arrived, I couldn't speak, but at least by then I knew the things I mustn't say. I knew it was better not to speak at all than to say the wrong things.

So I became mute.

Hoc opus, hic labor est.

My blabbing mouth was silent.

It was as if I had some terrible disease.

I was hustled from that room to a taxi and out of the country.

I used to wonder what the other girls were told about my sudden disappearance. Some silly lie, I presume. Harmless lie, they might have called it.

What did she say to Eddie?

I have wondered so often about that.

I used to imagine her sitting at her desk, writing those words to him.

What words?

Then lifting her head and staring out at the landscape.

Our landscape.

His and mine and Nellie's and father's and all those boys and girls with whom we had danced.

He never came.

He never wrote.

She didn't know the truth to tell him.

Perhaps she never told him anything and he was too busy being a soldier to care.

Too busy preparing himself for death.

Playing at being grown up with Wilkinson.

I always hoped he didn't hate me.

D-Day plus two.

She didn't tell me, of course.

She probably couldn't bring herself to write those words.

Darling Flora, Eddie is dead. You are all I have left in the world now. You must come home. You must bring the baby home.

How idiotic I am to think that she could have lifted her pen to write such words. It wasn't Eddie and I that did that thing.

It was they. The lovers. The dancers. It wasn't Eddie and Flora. When I could speak again, after it was all over, after death, after they had taken away the child, I tried to tell them.

I spoke to them. Then, I cried. I told them and told them over and over and over and they wouldn't believe what I was saying.

Wouldn't.

I screamed and they put me into the darkness.

I waited for father to come and save me.

He never came.

He could have told them the truth.

I wished I had never started to speak.

I longed to cut out my blabbing tongue.

I called and called for father and he never came and then, one day, I remembered that he too was dead.

In the desert. El Alamein.

I longed to follow them wherever they had gone. But no one would let me.

It's for your own good. What was good? Where would I ever find good?

I cried when they told me that the baby was a boy.

I never saw him, but I cried because I knew that somewhere a war would be waiting for him also. A beast of prey.

For your own good they said when I begged to see him. It's all for your own ...

I sometimes think I'm making all this up.

Sometimes, when I hear the song and the child crying, I whisper to myself it isn't true. None of this happened.

They were right. I was a girl unhinged by sorrow.

I am a mad old woman who doesn't know truth from fantasy.

I begged to hold him, even for a moment, in my arms, to whisper in his ear 'I love you', so that he would hold those words in his head forever.

But I never saw any of them again.

Chicken, I will love you forever.

Never.

[*She laughs. Throws her head back and laughs.*]

What a stupid, maudlin old woman I am.

This all such old grief.

They were never unkind.

Pills, potions, injections and my tongue swelled up in my mouth so that I couldn't babble.

When you get well you may go home.

Your poor mother can't handle this folly.

Think of your poor mother.

When you become well ...

When you no longer scream those lies.

When you learn to keep your mouth shut ... Button your lip. Nellie!

They still keep an eye on me. Dr. Carey ... those guardians, trustees, whatever you like to call them.

Mustn't ever let them see me like this.

Not very often babbling these days.

Only those anniversaries, birth days, death days. Parting days.

Nellie tries to keep them from me, but she is transparent, like a pane of glass. Even in the early morning when she wakes me with a cup of tea, I can see it in her face.

This is one of those days. We may have a little trouble today.

Poor, dear Nellie.

Nellie!

I've lost the use of my legs. I can't stand up.

Nellie! Where are you?

NELLIE'S VOICE: Coming. Coming. [*She comes in carrying a tray.*]

I've made a nice cup of tea and I put a bottle in your bed. That's what kept me. It'll be nice and warm by the time you tumble in.

FLORA: I've lost the use of my legs.

NELLIE: Of course you haven't. It's all that drink. I was hard put to it in the kitchen to find the kettle. We're a terrible pair of old soaks. You'd think we'd have learned a bit of sense at our age.

FLORA: Conisurios.

NELLIE: That makes it better all right. A better class of soak. There's your tea now. Drink it up while its nice and hot. We'll be fit for nothing in the morning. And I'll tell you what we never did, with all that blathering ... we never named our horses. Where's that paper now, till I have a look?

[*She looks around for the paper and when she finds it she settles down at the table with a pen in her fist.*]

Kempton. Fairyhouse. Lingfield.

One o'clock. Kempton. Nothing much to write home about there.

Can Can Charlie, Desert Challenger.

If you're going to drop off put that cup on the table or you'll have it all over your clothes.

Captain Marmalade, Danny Gale, Jet Boys.

I like the sound of Captain Marmalade. That's a droll name. It speaks to me, that name. Five to one. We might put a quid on Captain Marmalade. Huh?

[*As she speaks the sound of* 'Lili Marlene', *very softly, can be heard.*]

FLORA: Each way.

NELLIE: Each way. That's one decision made anyway. Macushla. Tribal Boy. No, no.

You know, I think I need glasses. I'm finding it very hard these days to see the small print. I wonder should I have a word with Dr. Carey when he comes next . The letters slither away from me sometimes. Maybe it's the wine. What do you think? Does too much wine affect the eyes? It's probably age. That's what he'll say. We're not getting any younger, Nellie.

Silly thing to say really when you think about it. Don't we spend our lives not getting any younger?

Paperchase. Captain X. Champagne Charlie.

[*She laughs.*]

That sounds like the one for us. Not much form, though. I think we might be throwing our money away. Think how cross we'd be, sitting here tomorrow afternoon watching Champagne Charlie coming in last.

FLORA: Nellie.

NELLIE: Mmm?

FLORA: Did you ever name the stars?

NELLIE: Name the stars?

FLORA: Yes. Film stars names. You remember you told me ...

NELLIE: Never got round to doing that. You're not concentrating. I think we'd better leave this to the morning, when my eyes are working and I can see the names and you can concentrate. That's another decision made anyway.

Yes, I remember now, I always wanted to do that. Spend a whole night naming the stars. Dear God, that was all such a long time ago. So much childishness in the head. And innocence. Wasn't that pure innocence?

FLORA: I was thinking, we might do it some night together. Some great clear night, when you can see them all. We could put on our coats and go out and do that. You could teach me all those names. Judy Garland, Bette Davis, Fred Astaire. All those people. Perhaps we could sing their songs, talk about their stories. Drown the old tired voices in our heads.

NELLIE: Yes. I'd like to do that. Some night. I don't think Dr. Carey would have any complaints about that.

We mightn't tell him on the other hand. A little secret like. Another little secret. [*She laughs.*]

Mum's the word.

We'd have to wrap up well. The night cold gets into old bones. Yes. We might do that some night.

FLORA: What about tonight, Nellie? I'd like to do it now. Do something.

We never do anything, you and I.

[*She moves towards the window and opens it.*]

Look at them all up there. Waiting.

[*She steps out into the garden.*]

NELLIE: You'll get your death. Where's your ...? Some night I said ... let you ...

[*She is searching round the room for a wrap. The house fades slowly.* FLORA *stands in the garden looking up. There are a million stars.*]

FLORA: I can see Fred Astaire quite clearly up there ... Nellie, do come and see. Judy Garland, Gary Cooper ... oh and that great big one there ... Nellie. Look. What will we call ...?

[NELLIE *steps out from the house with a blanket which she gently puts around Flora's shoulders.*]

That one...? It must be a planet, it shines so brightly.

NELLIE: Bette Davis.

FLORA: Yes. Bette Davis.

[*The lights go slowly down and the singer sings on.*]

[*The end*]

Other Plays from Lagan Press

Joseph Tomelty
All Souls' Night & Other Plays
edited and introduced by Damian Smyth
ISBN: 1 873687 04 4
216 pp, £4.95 pbk

Best know as a stage and film actor and as the creator of *The McCooeys*—Northern Ireland's 1940s radio soap which made him a household name in his native place—Joseph Tomelty was also a novelist, short-story writer and, above all, a playwright.

This book, selected by the critic Damian Smyth, gathers for the first time into one volume four major Tomelty plays—the sombre and deeply sad *All Souls' Night* (1948), the lyric *The Singing Bird* (1948), the serio-comic *April in Assagh* (1953) and the controversial *The End House* (1944).

All Souls' Night, set in a dark, passionless world on the east coast of Ulster, is his most critically-acclaimed play. Dealing with poverty, meanness of soul and a mother's consuming greed, it has been described as the best play written in the north of Ireland. It is counterpointed by *April in Assagh*, a play set in a fantastical townland, which is funny and satirical with a dark core of foreboding and published here for the first time. *The End House* creates a Belfast of urban violence after the model of O'Casey. *The Singing Bird*, written for radio in 1948 and later adapted for television, starring Tomelty himself, is a beautiful, pastoral tale of 'a gentle madness'.

Together, these plays provide an indispensable insight into the workings of the double-sided imagination of Tomelty's place— one the one hand deeply obsessive and corrosive, on the other witty, meditative and happy and all with an exhilarating muscular lyricism.

Martin Lynch
Three Plays

Dockers • *The Interrogation of Ambrose Fogarty* • *Pictures of Tomorrow*
edited and introduced by Damian Smyth
ISBN: 1 873687 60 5
224 pp, £4.95 pbk

Martin Lynch has been a significant figure in Irish drama since the late 1970s when *They are Taking Down the Barricades* gave expression to contemporary Belfast working-class life. Rooted among the political and imaginative forces bearing upon and emerging from both northern communities, Lynch explored those forces with humour, anger and compassion.

Having committed himself to the values of community-based drama, he wrote a string of popular successes throughout the 1980s. Marked by an accurate ear for dialogue and a pungent wit, the plays chalked out a territory securely his own. Out of this commitment have come also three of the most important plays in the last twenty-five years from the north of Ireland—*Dockers, The Interrogation of Ambrose Fogarty* and *Pictures of Tomorrow.*

Dockers is a boisterous recreation of working-class life in Belfast's famed Sailortown district. Reminiscent of Dario Fo but rigorously rooted in the sadness of real political conflict, *The Interrogation of Ambrose Fogarty* is a most vivid, pointed and funny play dealing with the ironies and absurdities of police detention. With *Pictures of Tomorrow*, Lynch attempts to deal with the disillusion of left-wing ideals in the wake of the collapse of communism, against the poignant backdrop of the Spanish Civil War, a conflict loaded with Irish resonances.

These plays, available for the first time, establish Martin Lynch as a leading Irish playwright of his generation.

Jennifer Johnston
Three Monologues
Twinkletoes • *Mustn't Forget High Noon* • *Christine*
ISBN: 1 873687 70 2
72 pp, £4.95 pbk

Collected for the first time in print, these monologues represent one of the many dimensions of the talent of Jennifer Johnston, one of Ireland's most important writers since the war.

Revolving round the griefs and traumas caused by the troubles in the north of Ireland, they are an exploration of individual survivals in the midst of the disintegration of life and lives.

Twinkletoes is the story of Karen, a top IRA prisoner's wife; looked up to by her community, she cannot express her loneliness. *Mustn't Forget High Noon* introduces Billy Maltseed, a border Protestant, who has just lost his best friend, a UDR part-timer, shot by the IRA. In *Christine*, Billy's southern Irish wife mourns his death by violence which leaves her alone and childless in a community riven by suspicion.

These monologues—by turns comic and intensely moving—together reclaim the individual voice in the teeth of stereotypes, express most vividly the human beneath the inhuman and the headlines.

To order these or other Lagan Press titles, write to:
Lagan Press, PO Box 110 Belfast, BT12 4AB
(*post & packaging free*)